# Credit
# Freedom

# Credit
# Freedom

## SELF-CREDIT REPAIR IN TEN EASY STEPS

**Alvin Perkins**

ISBN: 1536913944
ISBN 13: 9781536913941
Library of Congress Control Number: 2016912943
CreateSpace Independent Publishing Platform
North Charleston, South Carolina

# Author's Note

I took the time to write this guide on credit in an attempt to reduce the average person's needless stress and worries about his or her credit situation. If you have good credit, then you can basically have anything you want without ever being denied. We all need good credit for everything from purchasing a house or a new car, to getting loans, and so forth. I once went to a free meeting to discuss how to better my credit scores with all three bureaus. I was given just enough information to pique my interest, and then the big sell came. They informed me that for $799, they could sell me exclusive information that I could find at the local library for free. Crazy, right? After lots of research, I have compiled this information for you, which won't get you rich but will help ease the tension in your mind and give you credit freedom. The following is a cheap-and-easy way to fix your credit scores with all three bureaus.

Good luck!
Alvin Perkins

# Notes from Experience

1. Because the credit bureaus handle millions of files, the possibility for error is substantial.
2. Write or call all four of the major credit-reporting agencies to request a copy of your credit report.
3. Find the negative remarks or "dings" in your credit report and circle them.
4. For future reference, make copies of all information sent to agencies.
5. Mail letters of dispute "registered certified" in order to obtain verification of receipt for your records.
6. The credit bureau will only verify the facts if you assert that they are in error.
7. It is frequently possible to eliminate negative marks simply by going through this process of disputing entries.
8. Be persistent! The only way to get what you want with the credit agencies is to bug the hell out of them.
9. Remember that credit can't be rebuilt in a day. It takes time and persistence.
10. The only limitation to your dispute of information in your credit report is that it should not be frivolous or irrelevant.

# Contents

# Five Common Reasons for Credit Denial

1. DELINQUENT CREDIT OBLIGATIONS: Late payments, bad debts, or legal judgments against you make you look like a risky customer.

2. INCOMPLETE CREDIT APPLICATIONS: Perhaps you left out some important information or made an error on an application. Any large discrepancy between your application and your credit file can count against you. The lender will wonder whether you are hiding something.

3. TOO MANY INQUIRIES: Inquiries are made whenever you apply for credit. Seeing your own report also counts as an inquiry, but that is usually not held against you. At the creditor's discretion, as few as four inquiries within six months may be considered a sign of excessive credit activity. The creditor may then presume that you are trying desperately to get credit and are being rejected elsewhere.

4. ERRORS IN YOUR FILE: These may arise simply from typing mistakes or from your name being confused with someone else's similar name. If you have changed your address, this can also create problems in the recording of your credit history. Because the credit bureaus handle millions of files, the possibility for error is substantial. Errors are found and corrected only through careful review of your file for accuracy, followed by the taking of necessary steps to correct any errors that are discovered.

5. INSUFFICIENT CREDIT HISTORY FILE: Your credit history is too scant for the type or amount of credit you request. You need to develop your credit history more fully before qualifying for the level of credit you are now requesting.

# What's in your Credit Report?

Credit reports may vary from agency to agency, but most include the following:

AN ACCOUNT LISTING: This includes the name of the issuer, the date the account was opened, the original balance and/or credit limit, the current balance (beginning with the reporting date, which is also listed), the terms of the account, and the status of the account. This leaves little room for guesswork. It also leaves little room for paying delinquent accounts and, therefore, for changing the status of your account, even if you are current.

YOUR PERSONAL INFORMATION: This includes your full name, your last two addresses, your Social Security number, your date of birth, and your place of employment (if the credit bureau has received that information). Length of employment and income are typically not reported, but watch for information on the former. When it is reported, length of employment is often incorrect. Creditors will sometimes reject an application because they can't confirm employment. If you are self-employed, credit bureaus may have you listed as unemployed, which should be corrected immediately.

PUBLIC RECORD INFORMATION: This includes bankruptcies, tax liens, judgments, and their filings, all of which are in the report.

CREDIT REPORT REQUESTS: Each time a creditor requests a copy of your report, the request is recorded in your report. This stays in your report for up to one year. This addition is "non-evaluated" by the bureau. Nevertheless, it can be seen negatively by creditors if you have too many inquiries within a short time. Creditors who see this will assume that you were turned down, even though there may be other explanations for the inquiries.

CONSUMER STATEMENT: Finally, there is space in the report for you to place a consumer statement. This allows you to challenge or explain in your own words any creditor entries in your file.

# STEP 1

# Identify your Credit Problems

Circle all negative remarks, or "dings," on your credit report. The report has a key for decoding the coded symbols used. Use them to understand what the report says about you.

## CHECK THE FOLLOWING:

A) Historical Status: Late payments come in thirty-, sixty-, and ninety-day periods. Many reasons can cause these to be automatically entered: the mail was late, a delay occurred in processing your payments, and so forth.

B) The Comments: Remarks such as "Charge-Off" and "Charge to P&L" (profit and loss) imply that you are a bad credit risk.

C) Inquiries: These are made by companies looking at your report for possible consideration of credit.

D) Public Record: This may appear in your credit report as tax liens, bankruptcies, or court judgments that affect you.

## STEP 2

# Score your Overall Credit

Somewhere on your credit report, you will find a column with a title such as "Account Profile." This column contains a summary rating for each of your accounts. It may read "Positive," "Negative," or "Nonrated." You will want to protest all negative and nonrated marks and eventually remove them from your report.

# STEP 3

## Draft a Protest to the Credit Bureaus Disputing each "Ding"

This is not the time to be shy. You must assert your legal rights. You must aggressively challenge any negative remarks on your report. You have that right under the Fair Credit Reporting Act (FCRA), 15 USC Section 1681i. (For every dispute you list, you must have a reason for the discrepancy.)

# STEP 4

# Send your Letter of Dispute

Using the letter templates provided in this publication (hereafter referred to as letters), write to the credit bureaus. Be sure to include photocopies of any documents that support your claims. Examples include canceled checks and receipts.

# STEP 5

## Record your Actions

Log the date for each letter or transaction between you and the agencies. Keep accurate information about what was deleted and from which agency. Maintain a good filing record because it may come in handy in the future.

# STEP 6

# Wait a Reasonable Time for a Response

Don't tolerate a delay of more than eight weeks for a reply. The waiting periods will depend on several factors. See letters for suggested time. Mark the dates down in your calendar.

**STEP 7**

# Send Follow-Up Letters

I f the agencies fail to respond, this may work in your favor. Write a follow-up letter (provided), and point out the fact that federal law requires the credit bureau to respond to a consumer dispute within a reasonable amount of time, and if not, the agency is in default.

**STEP 8**

# Ask for an Updated Credit Report

At the end of the letter, there should be a request for an updated copy of your credit report. By law, you should receive free notifications of any updates, but only when you request them.

# STEP 9

# Repeat the Process

Once you receive the updated report, compare it with previous ones. Make a note of the changes that were made. Notice whether the rating was upgraded from negative to nonrated to positive or deleted altogether. Chances are that you will not get results on every protest the first time, but some progress is likely.

There will probably still be some bad marks remaining. Be aware that a dispute can result in an even more negative rating than before. For example, unreported late payments may now be reported.

Now is the time to go back to the beginning of the process and start over. You should put your credit report through this process at least twice.

# STEP 10

# Do Not Give Up Until you See and Receive Results

Be persistent! Many people simply give up when they have not received any results. Repeat the steps over and over again until the desired results take place. Be a pest and *don't stop until it's done*. Remember: if at first you don't succeed, try, try again.

# Getting a Copy of your Report is Easy

t is easy to get copies of your records from those credit bureaus that have a report on you. The addresses of local offices can be found on the Internet under the search for credit rating and reporting.

Here is a list of the most frequently used agencies:

EQUIFAX
www.equifax.com
P.O. Box 740241
Atlanta, GA 30348
1-800-685-1111: Credit report inquiries
1-888-766-0008: Place fraud alerts on your credit report
1-866-493-9788: Credit reports, scores, and identity-theft monitoring

EXPERIAN
www.experian.com
P.O. Box 4500
Allen, TX 75013
1-888-397-3742: Credit report/dispute information/fraud identity and identity theft
1-877-284-7942: Triple advantage credit-monitoring membership
1-888-243-6951: Business credit services

TRANSUNION
www.transunion.com
P.O. Box 2000
Chester, PA 19022
1-800-493-2392: Credit-monitoring service inquiries
1-800-888-4213: Purchase a credit report or get a free annual report
1-800-916-8800: Dispute items on credit report and status checks
1-800-680-7289: Fraud alerts and identity-theft information
1-866-922-2100: Business services assistance
1-855-617-1318: Free credit-score summary and consultation

Write or call all three of the major credit reporting agencies listed above to request a copy of your credit report. Typically, they charge for this service. (By law, you are allowed to receive one free credit report a year from each of the three credit agencies.)

# Getting Help from your Creditor

After several attempts at removing negative remarks from your credit report, you may find that some can't be deleted or upgraded. The next best thing to do is to try to pursue your creditors to change their view of you—to lighten up. Here are several ways to get them on your side.

## Make contact

Write to each creditor explaining the reason for your problem. Be specific. Give details and provide documentation. Remind the creditor that you eventually paid your debt, and mention that you appreciate his/her/their services or products in spite of the payment problems that arose. Ask that the bad remarks be removed now that the account is settled. Also, ask creditors to send a statement to the credit bureaus stating that you are paid up.

## Keep accurate records

Make up a worksheet for each creditor that includes the account number, credit remarks, credit agency identification, and dates of communication.

## Phone them

Get up close and personal. They need to interact with a real person, not a letter. If at first you don't succeed, try, try again. With each attempt, you may get a person more positive or receptive than the last.

## Send your statement to the credit bureau

By law, you can send a statement to the credit bureau and ask for your consumer statement to be added to your file. You have that right per 15 USC Section I(b) of the Fair Credit Reporting Act.

## Persistence

Wait a few months and repeat the process. After some time, things may have changed at the creditor's office. Remember: if at first you don't succeed, try, try again.

# Sample Request Letters

**DATE:**

**ADDRESS:**

**RE: FINAL FOLLOW-UP ON FAILURE TO RESPOND**

To whom it may concern:

On_____, 20__, I sent you a follow-up letter pointing out that you had failed to respond to my disputes of certain items found on my credit report issued by your company. Copies of that letter and the original dispute letter are attached.

As of today, _____, 20__, you still have not fulfilled the intent and letter of the Fair Credit Reporting Act that requires your bureau, as a consumer-reporting agency, to maintain and ensure that information, as stated in said act, "is fair and equitable to the consumer."

Also, the law stipulates that bureaus will maintain "accuracy, relevancy, and proper utilization of such information" (15 USC Section 1681(e)).

You have not given me evidence that you have acted in a prompt or "fair and equitable" manner because none of the following requirements have been met:

1.  You have not submitted evidence of the investigation by giving me the names and addresses of persons contacted, nor have you removed from my report anything found to be inaccurate.
2.  You have not removed any item for which no verification could be found within the thirty-day reasonable-time rule.
3.  You have not taken care to maintain the accuracy, relevance, and proper use of information in my file.

I still dispute the items given in my attached letter. I expect an appropriate response on or before _____, 20__, for each item. Otherwise, I must contact the Federal Trade Commission.

I also expect the names and addresses of individuals you contact to verify the information so that I may follow up on any item.

Sincerely,

Name (printed)
Address, City, State, Zip
Social Security Number

**DATE:**

**ADDRESS:**

**RE: EXPLANATION FOR DELINQUENCY**

To whom it may concern:

It has recently come to my attention that several of my payments to your account are labeled "late" on my credit report.

I have been prompt in paying in the past, and missed the payments due to...

[Explain reason for delinquency.]

Since the late payments occurred for the above excusable reason, please correct the payment history for my account at the following credit bureaus, which carry your account histories:

[List credit bureaus.]

It is important that my credit report reflect the good relationship I have had with your company in the past. The corrections in the credit report will make it more representative of my financial habits.

I appreciate your assistance.

Sincerely,

Name (Printed)
Address, City, State, Zip
Social Security number

**DATE:**

**ADDRESS:**

**RE: DEMAND FOR CORRECTED CREDIT REPORT**

To whom it may concern:

On _____, 20___, I wrote to tell you that I had not heard about any specific actions taken to verify the items I had identified as inaccurate or incomplete in my credit report. Copies of my correspondence are attached for your reference.

Because you have not given me names of persons you contacted for verification of the information nor have you complied within a "reasonable time" to my request for verification, I assume that you have not been able to verify the information I have disputed. Therefore, you must comply with the provision of the Fair Credit Reporting Act and drop the disputed items from my credit report.

I demand that you send me a copy of my updated credit report showing the elimination of the items that I disputed in the attached letters. According to 15 USC Section 1681(j), this copy must be provided free of charge. I demand that it be postmarked no later than five days after signing the certified-mail receipt for the letter you are holding.

If I do not receive an updated copy of my credit report with the disputed items dropped, my attorney will pursue my legal rights under 15 USC Section 1681i(n) or 1681i(o) of the Fair Credit Reporting Act, "Civil liability for willful noncompliance." Your credit bureau may be liable for

1. any action damages I sustain by your failure to delete the items;
2. punitive damages as the court may allow; and
3. the cost of the court action plus attorney's fees.

I have forwarded a copy of this letter to the Federal Trade Commission.

Sincerely,

Name (Printed)
Address, City, State, Zip
Social Security number

**DATE:**

**ADDRESS:**

**RE: CONSUMER STATEMENT**

To whom it may concern:

According to the Fair Credit Reporting Act 15 USC Section 1611i(b), I have the right to enter a "consumer statement" in my credit report. I have disputed the accuracy and completeness of the items circled in pen on the attached credit report.

Because reinvestigation has not resolved my dispute, I want the following statement to be included in my credit report, setting forth the nature of my dispute for others to see.

[Add statement here.]

According to the Fair Credit Reporting Act, please send me a free updated copy of my credit report with the above statement included.

I will assume that thirty days represent a "reasonable time" for completing this update, unless you immediately notify me of any delays.

Sincerely,

Name (Printed)
Address, City, State, Zip
Social Security Number

**DATE:**

**ADDRESS:**

**RE: REQUEST TO UPDATE ACCOUNT**

To whom it may concern:

I recently received my credit report and located problems of inaccurate reporting. A copy of the credit report is attached with the disputed item numbers marked.

Under the provisions of the Fair Credit Reporting Act 15 USC Section 1681i, please reinvestigate and delete these disputed items. Send me the names and addresses of persons contacted. Unless you immediately notify me otherwise, I shall assume that thirty days constitute a "reasonable time" to complete these actions. It shall be understood that failure to verify within this time constitutes nonverification and that, according to Section 1681i(a), the items must be promptly deleted from my report.

Also, pursuant to 15 USC Section 1681(d) of the Fair Credit Reporting Act, please notify me when the items have been deleted. Send an updated copy of my credit report to the address below. According to 15 USC Section 1681i(j), there is no charge for notification of changes in my credit report.

Sincerely,

Name (Printed)
Address, City, State, Zip
Social Security Number

**DATE:**

**ADDRESS:**

**RE: REQUEST TO DELETE ACCOUNTS**

To whom it may concern:

I recently received my credit report and located problems of inaccurate reporting. A copy of the credit report is attached. The item numbers in question are marked in pen on the report.

Under the provisions of the Fair Credit Reporting Act, 15 USC Section 1681i(a), please investigate and delete these disputed items. Send me the names and addresses of persons contacted. I shall assume that thirty days constitute a "reasonable time" to complete these actions unless you immediately notify me otherwise. It should be understood that failure to verify within this time constitutes nonverification and that, according to Section 1681i(a), these items must be promptly deleted.

Also pursuant to 15 USC Section 1681(d) of the Fair Credit Reporting Act, please notify me when the items have been deleted. Send an updated copy of my credit report to the address below. According to 15 USC Section 1681(j), there is no charge for this notification of changes in my credit report.

Sincerely,

Name (Printed)
Address, City, State, Zip
Social Security Number

**DATE:**

**ADDRESS:**

**RE: REQUEST FOR FREE CREDIT REPORT**

To whom it may concern:

According to the attached letter, which states that my credit application was denied by_____, your credit bureau issued the report that was used for my credit evaluation.

The Fair Credit Reporting Act of 1970, 15 USC Section 1681i(g), provides that the credit bureau used should send me the information that led to the denial of my credit application. According to the provisions of 15 USC Section 1681i(j), there should be no charge for this information.

Please send my credit report to the address below. Additional information identifying my account can be found on the attached letter sent to me by _____, who denied my credit application.

Sincerely,

Name (Printed)
Address, City, State, Zip
Social Security Number

**DATE:**

**ADDRESS:**

**RE: REMINDER TO RESPOND**

To whom it may concern:

Thirty days ago you received my letter disputing several items listed in my credit report, issued by your firm. The item(s) are inaccurate and incomplete. I have attached the original letter.

Note that thirty days is considered a "reasonable time" under the Fair Credit Reporting Act 15, USC Section 1681i for responding to my request for verification of the erroneous items. Because you did not immediately write to inform me of the need for additional time, I presume that you accepted the thirty-day time limit.

I have not received a reply from you within these thirty days. Therefore, it must be that the information on my report is either inaccurate or it cannot be verified. In either case, according to the provisions of 15 USC Section 1681i(a), the items must be deleted immediately.

Please respond to this letter immediately so that I do not need to pursue my legal rights under 15 USC Section 1681(n) or 1681(o), which require your compliance to the law.

Also pursuant to 15 USC Section 1681(d) of the Fair Credit Reporting Act, please notify me when the items have been deleted. Send an updated copy of my credit report to the address below. According to 15 USC Section 1681(j), there is no charge for notification of changes in my credit report.

Sincerely,

Name (Printed)
Address, City, State, Zip
Social Security Number

**DATE:**

**ADDRESS:**

**RE: REQUEST FOR ADDITION OF SUPPLEMENTARY CREDIT HISTORY INFORMATION**

To whom it may concern:

Please include in my credit report the supplemental information attached. According to the Fair Credit Reporting Act [FCRA], 15 USC Section 1681(b), "It is the purpose of this title [FCRA] to require that consumer reporting agencies adopt reasonable procedures for meeting the needs of commerce for consumer credit, personnel, insurance, and other information in a manner which is fair and equitable to the consumer, about the confidentiality, accuracy, relevancy, and proper utilization of such information according to the requirements of this title." The intent of the FCRA includes recording supplementary credit information if requested by a consumer.

Accordingly, I hereby request that you add the attached history of payments, under the FCRA, 15 USC Section 1681(e) requirements that a consumer's credit report should reflect "completeness and accuracy" within a "reasonable" time after notification by the consumer.

Sincerely,

Name (Printed)
Address, City, State, Zip
Social Security number

**DATE:**

**ADDRESS:**

**RE: REQUEST TO MERGE INQUIRY WITH ACCOUNT**

To whom it may concern:

I recently received my credit report and located problems of inaccurate reporting. A copy of the credit report is attached with the item numbers marked.

[Describe.]

The presence of the inquiries as entries separate from the resulting accounts inaccurately duplicates information. The inquiries reflect an incomplete and inaccurate processing of information in my file. The inquiry entries should be removed or at least merged into the accounts to which they belong.

Under the provisions of the Fair Credit Reporting Act 15 USC Section 1681i, please investigate and delete these disputed items. Send me the names and addresses of persons contacted. I shall assume that thirty days constitute a "reasonable time" to complete these actions unless you immediately notify me otherwise. It shall be understood that failure to verify within this time constitutes nonverification and that items must be promptly deleted according to Section 1681i(a).

Also pursuant to 15 USC 1681(d) of the Fair Credit Reporting Act, please notify me when the items have been deleted. Send an updated copy of my credit report to the address below. According to 15 USC Section 1681j, there is no charge for notification of changes in my credit report.

Sincerely,

Name (Printed)
Address, City, State, Zip
Social Security number

**DATE:**

**ADDRESS:**

**RE: REQUEST FOR FREE CREDIT REPORT**

To whom it may concern:

Per your policy of one free credit report per year, please send me a copy of my report to the below address.

Sincerely,

Name (Printed)
Address, City, State, Zip
Social Security Number

**DATE:**

**ADDRESS:**

**RE: REQUEST FOR CREDIT REPORT**

To whom it may concern:

Please send me a copy of my credit report.
Enclosed is $_____ as payment for the credit report.

Sincerely,

Name (Printed)
Address, City, State, Zip
Social Security Number

**DATE:**

**ADDRESS:**

**RE: COMPLAINT LETTER TO DELETE INFORMATION**

To whom it may concern:

I received a copy of my credit report and found the following items to be in error. See the attached copy of the credit report, with the following item numbers written beside the problem entries.

[Describe.]

By the provisions of 15 USC Section 1681i of the Fair Credit Reporting Act of 1970, I demand that these items be investigated and deleted from my record. Send me the names and addresses of individuals you contacted so that I may follow up.

Unless you immediately notify me otherwise, I shall assume that thirty days constitute a "reasonable time" for verification of these entries. According to Section 1681i(a), any notification later constitutes reason to promptly drop the information from my file.

Also pursuant to 15 USC Section 1681i(d) of the Fair Credit Reporting Act, please notify me when the items have been deleted. You may send an updated copy of my credit report to the address below. According to the provisions of 15 USC Section 1681j, there should be no charge for this notification.

Sincerely,

Name (Printed)
Address, City, State, Zip
Social Security Number

**DATE:**

**ADDRESS:**

**RE: REQUEST FOR ADDITION OF SUPPLEMENTARY CREDIT HISTORY INFORMATION**

To whom it may concern:

Please include in my credit report the attached supplemental information.

According to the Fair Credit Reporting Act [FCRA], 15 USC Section 1681(b), "It is the purpose of this title [FCRA] to require that consumer reporting agencies adopt reasonable procedures for meeting the needs of commerce for consumer credit, personnel, insurance, and other information in a manner which is fair and equitable to the consumer, about the confidentiality, accuracy, relevancy, and proper utilization of such information according to the requirements of this title." The intent of the FCRA includes recording supplementary credit information if requested by a consumer.

Accordingly, I hereby request that you add the attached history of payments, under the FCRA 15 USC Section 1681(e) requirements that a consumer's credit report should reflect "completeness and accuracy" within a "reasonable" time after notification by the consumer.

Sincerely,

Name (Printed)
Address, City, State, Zip
Social Security Number

**DATE:**

**ADDRESS:**

**RE: CONSUMER STATEMENT**

To whom it may concern:

According to the Fair Credit Reporting Act, 15 USC Section 1611i(b), I have the right to enter a "consumer statement" in my credit report. I have disputed the accuracy and completeness of the items circled in pen in the attached credit report.

Because reinvestigation has not resolved my dispute, I want the following statement included in my credit report in order to set forth the nature of my dispute for others to see.

[Add statement here.]

According to the Fair Credit Reporting Act, please send me a free updated copy of my credit report with the above statement included.

I assume that thirty days represent a "reasonable time" for completing this update, unless you immediately notify me of any delays.

Sincerely,

Name (Printed)
Address, City, State, Zip
Social Security Number

**DATE:**

**ADDRESS:**

**RE: EXPLANATION FOR DELINQUENT PAYMENT**

To whom it may concern:

It has recently come to my attention that several of my payments to your account are labeled "late" in my credit report.

I have been prompt in paying in the past and missed the payments due to...

[Explain delinquencies.]

Because the late payments occurred for the above excusable reason, please correct the payment history for my account at the following credit bureaus, which carry my account histories:

[List credit bureaus.]

It is important that my credit report reflect the good relations I have had with your company in the past. The corrections in the credit report will make it more representative of my financial habits.

I appreciate your assistance.

Sincerely,

Name (Printed)
Address, City, State, Zip
Social Security Number

www.ingramcontent.com/pod-product-compliance
Lightning Source LLC
Chambersburg PA
CBHW040924180526
45159CB00002BA/597